Tell me, Master

Shri Ram Chandra Mission®
World Headquarters
Babuji Memorial Ashram
Manapakkam, Chennai 600 116
India
www.srcm.org

Compiled and illustrated by Veronique Nicolai
With the help of Elizabeth Denley

First Edition : 2006
Copies   : 8500

Printed in India at
Sudarsan Graphics
No. 27, Neelakanda Mehta Street
T. Nagar, Chennai 600017

ISBN: 81-7894-092-2

CONTENTS

What is God ?

Well, if I knew it, it would be very easy to answer that question, but nobody knows. My Master said, "God cannot be known because He is not an object. But His presence can be felt." Like you say you are happy but you cannot see happiness. Or like electricity, which makes the lights and fans and machines work, but you don't see electricity yourself. So, God is like that.

Is there really a Heaven?

It is not some place up there, you know, it is a state of existence. When we exist in a particular way, we say, "This is heaven." When we are sick and miserable, we say, "This is hell." Philosophers say heaven and hell are all here. So it is wrong to think that heaven is a certain place and hell is a certain place. We create hell or heaven by the way we live. For each person it is possible to have a heaven or a hell personally for himself or herself.

God

Is there a devil?

What do you think? No.

No. I think so too. There doesn't have to be a devil. I think these are stories taught to frighten us so that we don't do wrong things. In spirituality we believe that we should not frighten people into doing right, but teach them how to do right, persuade them how to do right.

What is the difference between man and God?

You know what water is – when it freezes it becomes ice; when it vaporizes it becomes steam, what you see in the clouds; when that becomes cold, it becomes rain. It's the same water. The ice is hard, cold and solid. That, you can say, is like the heart, the cold heart, which produces the lower forms of life. When it is just water, it is mobile, it can move, it has no particular shape, it takes the shape of anything that you put it into, and that is in between. And that which has no shape, no sound, no form, no colour, and which can technically be anywhere, like water vapour, is like God.

Babuji was very fond of this answer when I told him.

Why did God make India, Pakistan, China and other countries?

God did not make countries. He made the earth. Men divided it into countries and started fighting for the borders.

Since God made everything, why are there also bad things that God lets man do?

You see, here we must understand one thing clearly – God did not make bad things. We, people, make bad things. It's like you have a kid to play with you and you expect the child to behave well and to play in a cooperative spirit, in a friendly manner. But suppose that kid becomes quarrelsome and angry and throws things around? Will you blame God, or that particular kid? So we must learn to correct our own behaviour and become good, so that God cannot be blamed for our faults. God did not make wicked people. It is people who have become wicked by their wrong actions.

Is there ever going to be peace again? Will there be another war?

Well, at the moment we have peace of sorts. There are places where there is a little war here and there, but not war as we understand it. I hope there won't be another war. My Master has said, "It depends upon us."

War is not something that God brings down on us. If people behave senselessly, stupidly, and want to grab each other's territories and each other's property and wealth, then we have war. So please remember, it is people who create wars. You are all going to grow up into good citizens who must be able to control the destiny of your country.

Why are we ever born if we are just supposed to die and go to God?

Well, we are not born just to die to go to God. Life is supposed to be like a school. You go to school and, there, you can ask the same question. Why do we go to school if we are only going to get out of school at the end of it? You go to school to pass out of school, but in between you learn something. You learn what you have to learn or what you want to learn. You qualify yourself, isn't it? Similarly in life we qualify ourselves in certain ways, by living here, by experiencing things, by knowing things, and then, out we go. So, it is like a school classroom. We are not born just to die. You understand?

Why is there a feeling of sadness when we seek God?

It is not sadness but craving. When you are denied a chocolate, you feel the craving for it. When an older boy is denied a motorbike, he feels the craving for it. When still older, if he is looking for a girl to marry but does not find her, he feels unhappy. In the pursuit of God also such unhappiness (craving) results as long as you don't find Him. When you do find Him, there is no more unhappiness.

The adults often talk about the goal of Sahaj Marg. What is the Goal?

The goal is to become a perfect human being. One goes through three stages:

1. You want to be a good human being because Master loves you.

2. You want to be like the Master, externally.

3. Eventually you realize that it is no use being like the Master externally, for example in behaviour and looks, but we must be like the Master inside, spiritually.

Who invented the Sahaj Marg system of meditation?

We cannot say who invented it because when Lalaji Maharaj rediscovered it, he found that it was already there some five thousand years ago, during the time of the king Dasharath, who was Lord Rama's father. And how long it was there before that, nobody can say. So it was not invented – it was only rediscovered by our Grand Master.

There are lots of people who meditate. Why is Sahaj Marg different?

This is like asking, "There are so many people who eat. How is what you eat different?" Food is not different, but what we eat can be different. So meditation is meditation, but Sahaj Marg has its own speciality, which is not something different – what makes Sahaj Marg unique is its effectiveness in transforming people.

Mission

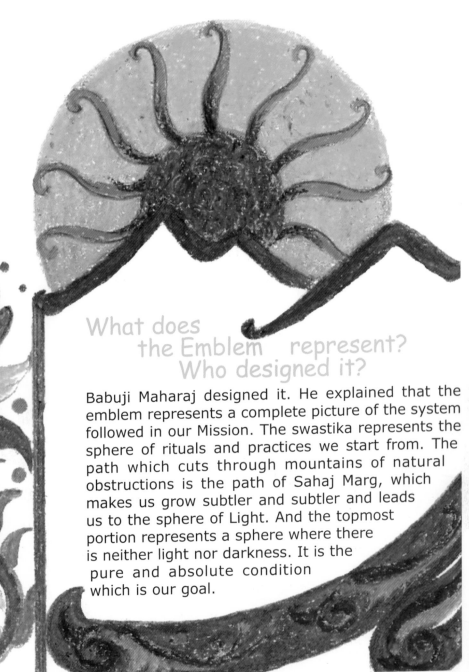

What does the Emblem represent? Who designed it?

Babuji Maharaj designed it. He explained that the emblem represents a complete picture of the system followed in our Mission. The swastika represents the sphere of rituals and practices we start from. The path which cuts through mountains of natural obstructions is the path of Sahaj Marg, which makes us grow subtler and subtler and leads us to the sphere of Light. And the topmost portion represents a sphere where there is neither light nor darkness. It is the pure and absolute condition which is our goal.

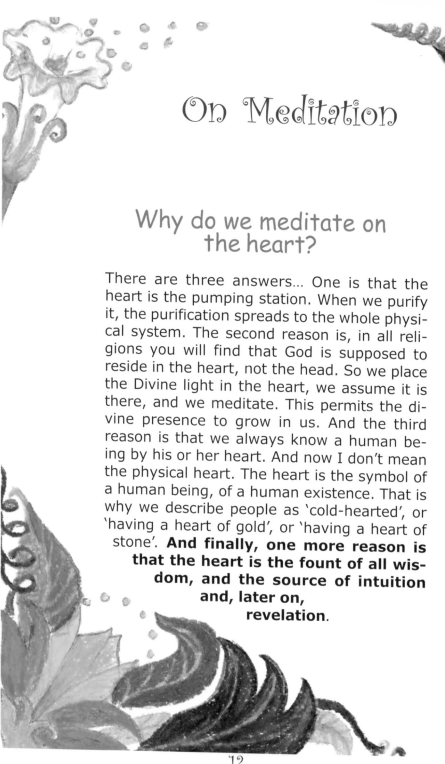

On Meditation

Why do we meditate on the heart?

There are three answers... One is that the heart is the pumping station. When we purify it, the purification spreads to the whole physical system. The second reason is, in all religions you will find that God is supposed to reside in the heart, not the head. So we place the Divine light in the heart, we assume it is there, and we meditate. This permits the divine presence to grow in us. And the third reason is that we always know a human being by his or her heart. And now I don't mean the physical heart. The heart is the symbol of a human being, of a human existence. That is why we describe people as 'cold-hearted', or 'having a heart of gold', or 'having a heart of stone'. **And finally, one more reason is that the heart is the fount of all wisdom, and the source of intuition and, later on, revelation**.

What does meditation bring?

Try it, when you are old enough. It is not possible to say. You see, somebody takes chocolate ice cream, someone wants vanilla, the third wants ice cream with nuts, but it's all the same. We have all these funny ideas about what we get, only when we think of getting and giving. When we think only of existing, there is nothing.

Why do we close our eyes to meditate?

Because if we keep our eyes open, we are going to be distracted by everything that passes in front of us and around us. In meditation we are supposed to look inside and try to have this idea that there is Divine light in the heart, and if we keep our eyes open we cannot do that.

Why do you need to clean yourself?

When we walk, our feet get dirty with the dust. If the place is very dirty, like if it has cow dung or slush after rain, it gets more dirty. The body also gets dirty with dust when we travel, so we have to clean the body. The mind gets similarly dirty because of unwanted thoughts that we have, and which leave their impression. Therefore cleaning is necessary.

What does one do while cleaning?

This is actually too difficult a question for children to understand, but you can say that like you put water over yourself to clean yourself and rub yourself briskly, so also you use the power of the Master to, in some way, wash the mind and clean up its unnecessary thoughts.

Cleaning

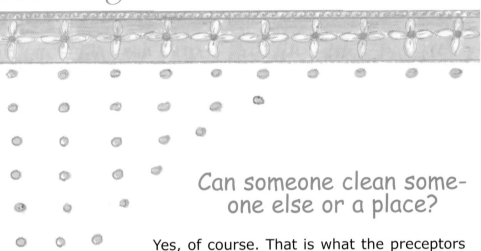

Can someone clean some-one else or a place?

Yes, of course. That is what the preceptors are doing all the time.

Where does everything go after the cleaning?

It is true that something has to go somewhere when it is not here. Now, where are your thoughts when you stop thinking? Physical matter occupies space. So we talk of something going somewhere which we have cleaned – like dirty water goes somewhere. But mental cleanliness does not deal with matter but with something else of a different dimension where there is no place or time. So we cannot say where it goes or when it goes, it just goes.

I remember a famous question which another child asked, "Mummy, mummy, where does the light go when the candle is blown out?"

What is praying? Our parents tell us to pray.

You should pray that whatever Master wants to happen will happen, not that which you want yourself. Not only do children pray for material things, adults do as well – and that is wrong. One should have patience – not demand a response to one's prayer but just wait, and then everything will follow on its own.

To whom should we pray?

Prayer should be addressed from the heart to the heart of the person to whom we are praying, because it is the heart which responds. According to Sahaj Marg, God has no mind. He is not a person, and therefore we advise that we pray to the Master himself, who has a heart which can respond to our prayer, if it is permitted.

What happens when we pray?

Well, we hope that what happens is what we pray for.

What is the correct way to do the 9 o'clock prayer?

Oh, just sit with your eyes closed and have the thought that all human beings are our brothers and sisters. It brings about human brotherhood somehow. It will come. We don't do it properly, so it doesn't come. We must put our **heart** into this thought, not our mind.

Can Children write a diary?

Children should be encouraged to write a diary. School children are encouraged to write a diary when they go out on an excursion. It is to train them in the habit of observation and to recall it. So it is a good habit for children to write a diary.

What should we write inside?

You should write what interests you. As your interests change, what you write will change.

On Samskaras

Are there good and bad samskaras?

No. Samskaras are samskaras. Can we have a good stomach ache or a bad stomach ache? Suppose a child eats chocolate and has stomach ache, while another child eats rotten food and has stomach ache. Can the rich child say, "My stomach ache is better than yours"? So there are no good samskaras, nor bad samskaras; there are only samskaras.

What is a 'Samskara'?

A samskara is the effect left behind of a thought or of an action. If somebody can think or do a thing without their leaving an effect or an impression on themselves, then there is no samskara.

19

Why are people afraid of death?

This is something so universal that nobody has found an answer to it yet. Philosophers say that death is the only thing that is certain. So how can we be afraid of it? People who believe in God say, "Well, we are all going to God. Why be afraid of death?" But, yet, everybody is afraid of it. It is because, after death we don't know what exists. So it is not exactly fear of death, but it is fear of the unknown that we have.

What is Liberation? What is Realisation?

Liberation is to be free from whatever is binding us to this worldly life. We think that our problems are binding us, our situations are binding us. But when we understand that we have created the situations ourselves, then we understand that we have to 'un-create' these things to liberate ourselves. In a spiritual

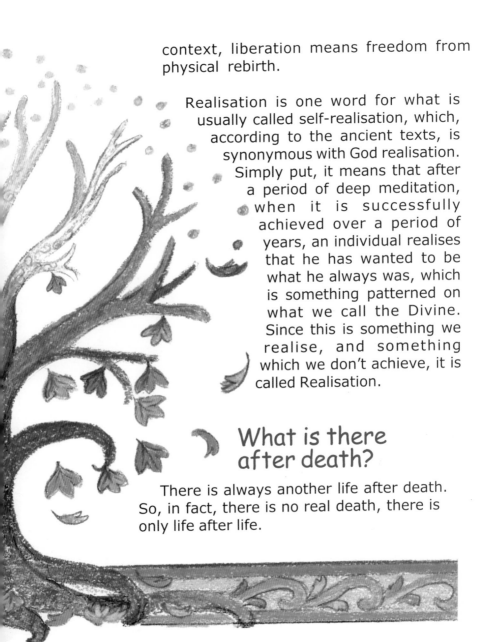

context, liberation means freedom from physical rebirth.

Realisation is one word for what is usually called self-realisation, which, according to the ancient texts, is synonymous with God realisation. Simply put, it means that after a period of deep meditation, when it is successfully achieved over a period of years, an individual realises that he has wanted to be what he always was, which is something patterned on what we call the Divine. Since this is something we realise, and something which we don't achieve, it is called Realisation.

What is there after death?

There is always another life after death. So, in fact, there is no real death, there is only life after life.

How can we fight fear?

No, no, we don't fight fear, because anything you fight will fight you. Just ignore. Suppose yesterday you were afraid of death, but you are alive today, so why continue to fear? We have been afraid of death every day, but we are still here. So what is the use of being afraid of death? Tell me.

How to develop the heart?

By giving up fear – because fear closes the heart.

How to give up fear?

This goes on, you know. [Laughs] How to give up fear? Give up fear. Babuji Maharaj has said every question has its own answer inside itself. How to abandon fear? Abandon fear. How to eat? Eat. It is very simple.

How do we know when we have opened the heart?

It is not something that is like a zipper, you know. You will know. When you can speak fearlessly. When you can speak only one thing – it is not the truth, it is not a lie. It is what it is. Then your heart is open.

How can we find this force [ability] within us?

It is there. You have not lost the force, but you are like a person who has the treasure in his house and doesn't know where it is. So in meditation, by cleaning, we find it again. We don't create; we uncover.

On
What

Love is what you feel when you look at your mother and when she looks at you. You can see it in her eyes.

When love alone can lead us to our goal, why do we need principles and books?

There are two things one must remember: you obey out of love and you obey out of rules and principles. One needs a balance.

Love

ove?

That is why we like to
think of the Master as
the mother, because
the Master is all
love.

Is it possible that Master knows about our love across distances?

Well, it must be so strong that He has to know
about it. Love cannot be ignored, if it is real love.
Not this mooching around, kissing behind the trees
– that's flirtation.

What is a Master?

A Master is someone who has mastered himself. Such a person is capable of using his mind and his body at his will. This means that he is no longer the slave of his mind, but he is the master of his own mind.

Why do we need a Master?

It is to help us master ourselves, so that we too can become like the Master.

How can we really benefit from the living Master?

Do what he advises you to do, first. I think that obedience is very, very important, and very efficacious. Obedience is most necessary and most effective. And it is also a sign of surrender when you can really obey.

Can the next Master be a woman?

No, it always has to be a man because a Master's work does not only deal with love. He must also be able to destroy. This a woman cannot do, because a woman's heart is only capable of loving. Their hearts can only work in a creative way. They cannot destroy, and the Master must be capable of loving as well as destroying. For that reason, it **must** be a man. It does not mean that women cannot become like their Master.

It is like that in Nature. This is why it was always the men who went to war and killed. Nowadays of course, there are more women becoming soldiers, but it would not be like that if we followed Nature. The Master must be capable of destroying the grossness which people have inside – evil, hatred, foolishness and ignorance.

As the number of abhyasis is growing, how will the relationship with the living Master be in the future?

The relationship is always there, you know. At the beginning it is a relationship between human and human (body to body), after that, heart to heart, and after that, spirit to spirit. That is all. Three levels we have. Each time it is the same. So we have the need for physical contact at the beginning of our spiritual work. But after some days, some weeks, some months, it is not necessary, if you have meditated properly, in the right manner – with love. If you love another person, physical contact is not necessary. In marriage also, there is the same problem. If you always have need of physical contact, you are at the level of a baby. Yes, mentally you are a baby, because the baby needs contact with the mother every moment. Isn't it? For adults it is not necessary, because we have the contact in our hearts – an interior contact.

Why do I have to wait until I am eighteen to start meditating?

You know, in Sahaj Marg we don't like kids to meditate before they are eighteen. In special cases we allow at sixteen. Children must be mature enough to know what they are doing and why they want to do it. That is why we don't like children to do it. There is another thing – you should not go too much into meditation and neglect your studies and your games. Children have to grow up with good bodies and good minds! Then they become fit for meditation. My Master used to say, "We want people like soldiers!"

How can I prepare myself to be an abhyasi later on?

There is a way to prepare yourself for this and that is to repeat the Mission's prayer once as soon as you wake up in the morning and once again just before you go to bed at night. In a couple of years, you will be so fit for Sahaj Marg that I shall invite you myself to start meditation.

Master and Me

To become like the Master, do you always have to stay with Him? If you cannot, what should you do?

Staying with Master is only part of it. You must have a craving to be like him.

How do you work on us children so that we will develop spiritually?

Sometimes I work on you, sometimes I wait. It is like all other kinds of work. Sometimes you are active, sometimes passive, but both are work. When, for instance, you sow a seed, you are not pottering about the soil all the time to see how the seed is doing. You have to wait. So you remain passive. Like when you boil potatoes! If anybody asks what you are doing, you will answer that you are waiting for the potatoes to get finished – which does not mean that you are doing nothing. You are waiting. What I mean is, while working, you are active as well as waiting.

Is there always going to be a living Master?

We hope so, but we cannot be sure of it – because for every family there is an end, when the family ceases to exist. Similarly, a line of Masters will exist as long as it is necessary, and then it will come to an end.

Could you speak about the role of children in Sahaj Marg?

You know, I would say 'the role of all the young people everywhere in the world'. I believe that the young have to create their world for themselves. What the elders did is finished with them. What today's adults are doing is wrong – not a good example for us. So they are useless. They don't set an example for us. They don't obey. So the children and the youth have to become capable of creating a new world. How can you create unless you are capable? We have to acquire the capacity, and this capacity is unique in a human being. It does not mean, you know, that the English are more capable, or the Germans, or the Indians. No, not at all. Every person has this capacity, but we use it in different ways; and when we use it in the wrong way, we lose the capacity. That is Nature's work. Nature will not give capacity in the wrong hands. Okay? Isn't it true?

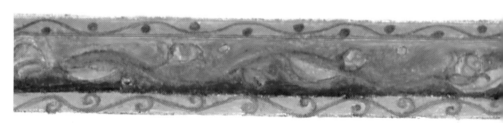

Future

My faith for the future is with the young. I work all the time because I have the faith of the youth. Adults work for themselves – not so the children. The children and the youth must work for the world, for the universe. The old people have become cynical. They don't have the vision that we need. They have lost their ide-alistic fervour. When we are young, we are capable of all these things. So even though the body may grow old, in the heart we must be young. Many people ask me, "How old are you?" My reply is always, "I am seventy-one years young." Yes, why not? When we are young, we don't lose faith. When we become old, we lose faith, we lose confidence, we have only selfishness. So we must re-main young in our heart all the time. The body becomes old, but not the heart. The heart is eternal.